CONTENTS

Around the world – the ultimate challenge   4

Ranulph Fiennes – to the ends of the Earth   10

Rick Hansen – around the world on wheels   16

Ellen MacArthur – going solo on the seas   22

Steve Fossett – circumnavigation by air   28

Jason Lewis – muscle power   36

Timeline   42

Quiz   43

Glossary   44

Find out more   46

Index   48

D0419758

AROUND THE WORLD
THE ULTIMATE CHALLENGE

Since the earliest times, humans have explored the world around them. They have asked questions such as "What's new to discover?" and "How far and how fast dare we go?"

Today, we can read books and watch films or TV programmes about famous explorers. We can also enjoy virtual adventures in fantasy worlds by playing computer games. If we're lucky, we get to go exploring on school trips or adventure holidays. We hope to see new sights, learn new skills, and find out more about the world we live in.

Then and now

The first journey around the world was made by Ferdinand Magellan and Juan Elcano. They set out from Spain in 1519, heading for Asia to buy valuable spices. Magellan was killed and many sailors died from disease, but Elcano and the survivors sailed on. They returned to Spain safely in 1522.

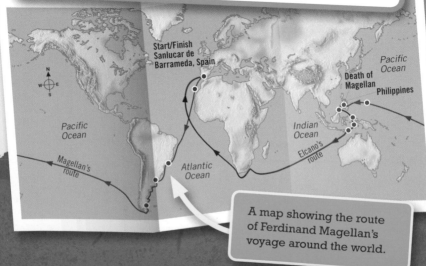

Start/Finish
Sanlucar de
Barrameda, Spain

Death of
Magellan

Philippines

Pacific
Ocean

Pacific
Ocean

Indian
Ocean

Elcano's
route

Magellan's
route

Atlantic
Ocean

A map showing the route of Ferdinand Magellan's voyage around the world.

S P R A Y

American sea-captain Joshua Slocum made the first-ever solo circumnavigation. His brave, lonely adventure took three years, from 1895 to 1898.

The ultimate adventure

A few special people go much further than this. They leave their homes, friends, and families, and they set out into the unknown on the greatest challenge imaginable – to travel right around the world. These brave men and women risk everything, sometimes even their lives, in pursuit of this achievement. Along the way they have adventures that test their minds, bodies, and spirits to the limit.

A new name

After Magellan's voyage, writers invented a new name for travelling right round the world: circumnavigation. They created it by joining together two Latin words: *circum* (which means "around") and *navigatum* (which means "sailed"). We use the same word today.

Exploration thrills! The trimaran *Earthrace*, steered by New Zealand adventurer Pete Bethune, claimed a new speed record (60 days) for circumnavigating the world in 2008.

A long way to go

Earth is a very big place. Its circumference is 40,075 kilometres (24,901 miles) at the Equator. If you could drive along the Equator at around 100 kilometres (65 miles) per hour, non-stop, all day and all night, it would take you almost 17 days to travel right around the world.

Of course you could not really do this. A lot of Earth's surface is covered by water, and even on dry land there are obstacles such as mountains, deserts, and ice-sheets. Overland, by sea, or in the air, any journey around the world is always difficult and often very dangerous.

Risks and dangers

As well as physical dangers, circumnavigators also face loneliness, stress, and sickness. For example, Magellan's sailors died from scurvy – a disease that made their teeth fall out and their flesh turn black with bruises. Solo voyager Slocum found his mind filled with disturbing images, and heard "the voices of the past, laughing, crying". Even so, circumnavigators all say that the excitement of their adventure makes the risks worthwhile.

TOOLS of the TRADE

Today, there are rules for circumnavigation. Adventurers must:
- start and finish at the same place
- keep going in the same direction
- cross the Equator and all lines of longitude
- pass places on exactly opposite sides of the world
- cover 40,000 kilometres (24,854 miles) or more.

Exploration spills! British adventurer Richard Branson crash-lands in North Africa during his bid to fly around the world in a hot-air balloon in 1997.

Fact and fiction

The earliest circumnavigators made their epic journeys by sea.
But in the 1800s, many new, faster, ways of travelling were invented.
These included steam-powered ships and locomotives.

In 1872, these new opportunities for fast travel inspired an exciting
adventure story. Called *Around the World in Eighty Days*, it was written
by French author Jules Verne and soon became a bestseller. Verne's
book tells how an eager but foolish Englishman, Phileas Fogg, sets off
on a race around the world. He is saved from many near-disasters by
his clever French servant, Passepartout.

In Jules Verne's story, the adventurers travelled by boat, train, and elephant. In the Oscar-winning film of Verne's book, they are shown flying by hot-air balloon as well.

Nouvelle Attraction

"I am feeling splendid … I am not in the least fatigued and have had good luck during my entire trip."
Nellie Bly, shortly after her safe return to the USA

Go, Nellie, go!

In 1889, a pioneering young newspaper reporter named Nellie Bly, from Burrell Township, Pennsylvania, USA, decided to see whether it was possible to travel around the world as fast as Jules Verne's storybook hero. To everyone's amazement, Bly completed the trip in just 72 days. She travelled by public transport, mainly steamships and railways. Nellie made this journey all alone, except for the pet monkey she took with her some of the way.

Nellie Bly, age 25, on her world trip. She carries everything she needs for her journey in one small handbag.

RANULPH FIENNES
TO THE ENDS OF THE EARTH

Called "the world's greatest living explorer", Ranulph Fiennes has taken part in dozens of adventures. In a career lasting almost 50 years, he has scrambled over glaciers in Norway, explored the River Nile by hovercraft, run seven marathons in seven days, discovered a lost city, and cut off his own frostbitten fingers.

Mad or marvellous?

Fiennes was born into an upper-class English family in 1944. He is distantly related to Queen Elizabeth II and to the actors Ralph and Joseph Fiennes. In 1970, he married his childhood sweetheart, Virginia (Ginny).

Ginny was an excellent organizer and fundraiser, and she shared Ranulph's love of adventure. Together, they planned a journey that no one had ever made before. They wanted to circumnavigate the globe from north to south, passing through both the North and South Poles. They called it the Transglobe Expedition. Prince Charles, a patron of the expedition, said the idea was "mad but marvellous"!

Fiennes attempted a solo expedition to the North Pole in 2000. He had to give up after his sleds fell through some ice and he got bad frostbite pulling them out.

Roald Amundsen

The first man to travel to both the South Pole and North Pole was the Norwegian explorer Roald Amundsen (1872–1928). However, Amundsen achieved this on two separate expeditions, 15 years apart – in 1911 and 1926.

Roald Amundsen's team catches seals during their expedition to the South Pole in 1911.

The Transglobe team

Ranulph and Ginny put together a support team of more than 30 men and women. From sea-captains to cooks, engineers, and electricians, each member had his or her own special skill. During the expedition Ginny worked as the radio operator, keeping the explorers in touch with the rest of the world. Without all these people, Fiennes's great adventure would not have been possible.

To the South Pole — and beyond

In 1979, Fiennes and fellow explorers Charlie Burton and Oliver Shepard set sail from London. After landing in France, the expedition drove through Europe and crossed the sea to Africa. There, they faced the Sahara Desert, with its searing heat, blinding sandstorms, and deadly poisonous scorpions. Next, they struggled through swamps and rainforests to Abidjan in Ivory Coast, where they boarded a ship for the Antarctic.

TOOLS of the TRADE

Fiennes's ship, the *Benjamin Bowring,* was designed for freezing seas. Its cabins were double-insulated. Its bow could smash through floating ice. Its strong steel hull was almost double the thickness of the hull of an ordinary boat. Spikes protected its rudder and propeller from icebergs.

The three main team members on the Transglobe Expedition – Shepard, Fiennes, and Burton – before they set out on their adventure in 1979.

A frozen world

The frozen landmass of Antarctica is a very dangerous place. It is always windy and extremely cold. Temperatures can stay below −20 degrees Celsius (−4 degrees Fahrenheit) even at the height of summer in December and January. The expedition route to the South Pole lay across deep crevasses and rock-hard lumps of ice.

Heading southwards

Fiennes, Burton, and Shepard now continued the journey alone. They travelled on skidoos, pulling sleds loaded with food and tents. Each man wore five layers of clothing – any uncovered skin would freeze in less than 30 seconds!

Fiennes and his companions finally reached the South Pole in December 1980. It was a great achievement, but they still had nearly 1,600 kilometres (1,000 miles) to cover. This would take them across treacherous glaciers, fragile snow-bridges, and steep mountain slopes. It was another four months before they finished crossing Antarctica and made it to Sydney in Australia.

Greenwich, UK

Sahara Desert

Cape Town, South Africa

Cape Town, South Africa

Antarctica

South Pole

Auckland, New Zealand

Sydney, Australia

North Pole

Los Angeles, USA

Greenwich, UK

The route of Ranulph Fiennes's Transglobe Expedition, 1979–1982.

13

Fiennes's dog, Bothie, went on some of the expedition. Afterwards, Ranulph and Ginny wrote a book about his journey!

The northward journey

At the end of the Antarctic crossing, Shepard went home, leaving Fiennes and Burton to journey north together on the *Benjamin Bowring*. They anchored off Alaska, USA, in June 1981. They had planned to travel north along the Yukon River, but fog and strong winds held them back. The two men had to wait in a camp for five months before the weather improved enough for them to continue their journey.

Close to death

In February 1982, still in killer cold, they set off for the North Pole on sleds and skidoos. But the Arctic sea had frozen into waves 12 metres (40 feet) high. Snowdrifts hid deep channels of sea-water in between ice-floes, and Fiennes's sled, loaded with equipment, fell down one! The explorers almost froze to death before a plane dropped fresh supplies.

Conquering Everest

In 2009, Fiennes became the oldest man to reach the summit of Everest – the highest mountain in the world. This feat made him the first person in the world to have climbed Everest and reached both poles.

Adrift on the ice

After reaching the North Pole in April 1982, Fiennes and Burton headed south. They got trapped on a large slab of floating ice, and drifted far out to sea. An agonizing 99 days passed before they were rescued by the team on board the *Benjamin Bowring*. The adventurers finally sailed back to England, where they were given a hero's welcome. They are the only people ever to have travelled around the world from north to south.

Never stop exploring: since the Transglobe Expedition, Fiennes has taken part in many more expeditions and has raised a great deal of money for charity.

RICK HANSEN

AROUND THE WORLD ON WHEELS

Rick Hansen was the first person to circumnavigate the globe in a wheelchair. He travelled a distance of 40,075 kilometres (24,902 miles), inspiring millions of people with his courage and determination.

Born in British Columbia, Canada, in 1957, Rick Hansen was a lively youngster who enjoyed sports and fishing. But when he was 15, a road accident changed Hansen's life. His spinal cord was damaged and his lower body was paralyzed. He could no longer walk or run.

Ball games

However, Hansen did not give up hope of being a sportsman. Instead, he learned how to play sports in his wheelchair. After university, he joined top wheelchair basketball and volleyball teams. In 1982, he took part in the Pan-American Wheelchair Games, where he won an amazing nine gold medals.

Hansen's epic around-the-world journey took him through 34 countries on four continents. Here, he wheels past the Eiffel Tower in Paris, France.

Rick Hansen has been an inspiration for disabled athletes for more than 25 years. In 2010, he carried the torch at the opening ceremony of the Winter Olympics.

Paralympic medallist

In the Paralympic Games in 1980 and 1984, Hansen competed for Canada as a long-distance wheelchair racer. More medals followed, and he became world wheelchair-marathon champion not just once, but four times. He was named Canadian Disabled Athlete of the Year in 1979, 1980, and 1982.

"I am driven by a deep passion and need to make a difference and leave this world a little better than when I arrived."
Rick Hansen

As a marathon racer, Hansen was used to tests of endurance, but in 1985 he set himself the greatest challenge yet. He wanted to wheel around the world!

A marathon journey

Most wheelchairs are not built for long-distance travel, but Hansen was young, strong, fit, and very determined. He longed for adventure. His family, his sports coach, and his friends all encouraged him in his plans. He was also inspired by his friend Terry Fox, a young athlete who died in 1981. Although seriously ill, Fox had spent the last months of his life running across Canada to raise money for medical research.

Hansen wheels along the Great Wall of China during his "Man In Motion" around-the-world adventure.

TOOLS OF THE TRADE

Hansen's wheelchair was specially built for his long expedition. This superlight chair weighed only 7.3 kilograms (16 pounds) – less than half the weight of an average wheelchair.

"Man In Motion"

Hansen's adventure, called the "Man In Motion World Tour", began in 1985 and took 792 days to complete. Hansen was on the move in his wheelchair for 465 of those days, and busy travelling across oceans in boats and planes for many more. Facing wind, rain, and sleet, Hansen wheeled his chair over snow and ice, and up and down mountain roads. He was chased by wild dogs, developed nasty sores, and caught dangerous infections. He had terrible pain in his hands, arms, and shoulders. He was robbed four times!

Keep rolling

On a typical day, Hansen rode for around eight hours, travelled over 80 kilometres (50 miles), and made 30,000 pushes of the wheels with his hands. He wheeled at speeds of around 14 kilometres (8.7 miles) an hour in the countryside. In the cities he travelled more slowly because of the crowds and the traffic.

However, there were also many high points on the journey. A rock musician wrote a song in Hansen's honour. Hansen received more than 200,000 letters of support. Admirers along the route showered him with roses. And he fell in love with expedition physiotherapist Amanda Reid, whom he later married.

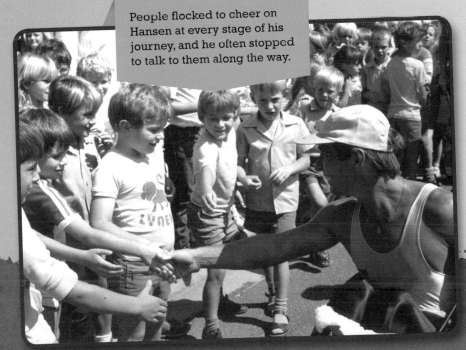

People flocked to cheer on Hansen at every stage of his journey, and he often stopped to talk to them along the way.

THE END IS JUST THE BEGINNING
Welcome Home Rick

24,_____MILE.S (40,000 KM.)

Thousands of people gathered in a stadium in Vancouver on 22 May 1987 to welcome Hansen home.

"If you believe in a dream and have the courage to try, anything is possible."
Rick Hansen

To help and inspire

Even during grim, pain-filled days, Hansen kept pushing the wheels of his chair round and round. Why continue his journey? Because he had a message to give to the world. He knew that people with disabilities were often ignored or neglected. He was determined to show what a wheelchair-user could achieve. Hansen refused to be invisible!

Everywhere Hansen went, he chatted to crowds, visited schools and colleges, and gave interviews. Sometimes he hardly had time to sleep. By the time he wheeled himself home to Vancouver, Canada, in May 1987, he had become a national hero and an international celebrity. He had survived an extraordinary around-the-world adventure that had pushed him to the limits of his endurance.

"The Hansen effect"

Today, Hansen uses his fame to raise money for good causes. His words and actions have inspired millions of people – supporters call this "the Hansen effect". Hansen still loves sport, especially fishing. He campaigns to protect the environment and to create "a healthier, more inclusive" world, not just for people in wheelchairs, but for everyone.

The *Lord Nelson* is equipped so that disabled and able-bodied sailors can work side by side to sail the ship.

Tall ship team

In 2012, a team of sailors with disabilities set off from London to travel around the world on a tall, fast, old-fashioned sailing ship. The ship is called the *Lord Nelson*, named after a British naval hero who lost one arm and one eye.

ELLEN MACARTHUR

GOING SOLO ON THE SEAS

Would you go without school lunch and save the money to buy a boat? Do you think you could make a solo voyage around Britain aged only 18? Would you be prepared to live for months in a shipyard shack, rebuilding a yacht for ocean racing? Champion sailor Ellen MacArthur did all that and more.

Born in 1976, in Derbyshire, England, MacArthur fell in love with boats during a family holiday to the seaside when she was just eight years old. She began to dream of sailing and of having wonderful adventures.

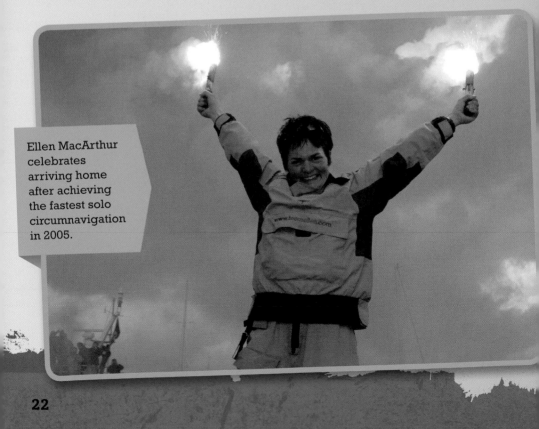

Ellen MacArthur celebrates arriving home after achieving the fastest solo circumnavigation in 2005.

Then and now

The first solo non-stop sailing circumnavigations were made by Britons Sir Francis Chichester in 1966–1967 (274 sailing days, with one break for urgent repairs) and Sir Robin Knox-Johnston in 1969 (non-stop 312 days). In 1988, Kay Cottee of Australia made the first solo non-stop circumnavigation by a woman (189 days).

It took Francis Chichester nine months and a day to sail around the world in his boat *Gipsy Moth IV*.

Early achievements

MacArthur's early career as a sailor was tough and often lonely. In 1997, three years after her brave around-Britain voyage, she raced solo across the Atlantic, covering 5,000 kilometres (3,100 miles) in just 33 days. In 1998, she came first for her class of boat in another transatlantic race – the gruelling Route de Rhum. Still only 22, MacArthur was honoured as "Yachtsman of the Year", a title given to the sailor who most impresses a team of expert judges. Suddenly, she was famous!

At one point in the race, MacArthur had to climb *Kingfisher*'s 15-metre (49-foot) mast to mend a sail, while the boat swayed wildly in huge waves.

The Vendée Globe challenge

MacArthur's fame led to sponsorship and a splendid new boat: the 9-tonne, single-hulled *Kingfisher*. In 2000, MacArthur set off in her sleek, fast new boat for the Vendée Globe around-the-world challenge. This was more than a long-distance ocean race. It was a life and death adventure!

Vendée competitors have to sail non-stop through the world's most savage seas, battling icebergs, storm-force winds, and waves that can reach 20 metres (65 feet) high. They must also cope with lack of sleep, exhaustion, and sheer terror! Accidents often happen – boats can be wrecked and sailors can break their arms and legs. Some have even died. MacArthur beat the odds and surged home after 94 days, in 2001. She was the youngest person and the fastest woman to have sailed around the world, non-stop, single-handed.

"It was the hardest challenge of my life, but I knew I had to do it."
Ellen MacArthur, on the 2000 Vendée Globe race

A team effort

MacArthur was extremely brave, strong-minded, and resourceful; she was also a very skilful sailor. But no one wins such achievements completely on their own. On both her around-the-world voyages, MacArthur was helped by an expert on-shore team made up of doctors, navigators, weather forecasters, psychologists, and nutritionists. They gave her advice by radio or through the internet.

MacArthur sits at the navigation station on board the *Kingfisher*.

Then and now

Before 2000, only one Briton had completed the Vendée Globe race: Pete Goss in 1997. The French have the best record in this challenge. In fact, in 1990 – the first time the race was held – only French sailors finished the journey.

A new challenge

In 2004, MacArthur was given a new boat, the trimaran *Castorama*, which was specially built for super-fast racing. The same year, French sailor Francis Joyon set a new world record for the fastest circumnavigation. MacArthur was determined to do even better. In November 2004, she set sail.

"An unbelievable journey"

At first, all went well, but soon after crossing the Equator MacArthur was almost killed by poisonous fumes from electrical equipment. She recovered, but her bad luck wasn't over. Huge waves forced her to change course, which lost her valuable time. Next, she faced violent storms and had to navigate around icebergs in the water. Sleepless and stressed, she injured herself in accidents, getting a bad burn and a nasty cut on the forehead. Even worse, she had to climb the swaying 30-metre (100-foot) mast to make repairs – twice!

By the time MacArthur reached home in February 2005, she was utterly exhausted. But she had beaten Joyon's record! She had made the fastest-ever solo voyage around the world: 71 days, 14 hours, 18 minutes, and 33 seconds.

MacArthur's record-breaking speedy route round the world in 2005.

TOOLS OF THE TRADE

The *Castorama* was 23 metres (75 feet) long and had three hulls. The wind blowing its huge sails powered it through the waves at 33 knots (61 kilometres) per hour. MacArthur described sailing at this speed as "like being on an [underground] train completely out of control."

MacArthur sails the *Castorama* in 2005. Safely back on shore, she said: "I don't think I will ever be able to communicate how difficult it has been."

STEVE FOSSETT

CIRCUMNAVIGATION BY AIR

Steve Fossett was a very successful businessman. He had made millions of dollars and could afford anything he wanted, but he felt restless and unhappy. He decided to start a new life full of adventure on land, in the air, and at sea.

As well as his achievements in aircraft, Fossett set 23 world records as a sailor.

Rutan and Yeager

The first non-stop flight around the world was a team effort by Dick Rutan and Jeana Yeager, from the United States. In 1986, taking it in turns to pilot their jet plane *Voyager* while the other slept, they made the trip in 9 days, 3 minutes, and 44 seconds.

A life-changing decision

Fossett was born in Jackson, Tennessee, USA, in 1944, but he grew up in California. He became a keen boy scout, and first climbed a mountain when he was only 12 years old. He went on to become a financial trader, and was extremely good at his job. He became very wealthy. However, 30 years later, Fossett still remembered the fun and the thrill of his early outdoor adventures. He decided he wanted more from his life.

Record-breaker

He learned to pilot different types of aircraft, from hot-air balloons to jet planes. He became a world-class yachtsman. He went cross-country skiing, dashed over the ice in sleds pulled by husky dogs, raced fast cars, ran marathons, swam the English Channel, and even planned to explore deep oceans in solo submarines. A keen competitor, Fossett eventually won 113 world records for extreme sports achievements – and three more for circumnavigations.

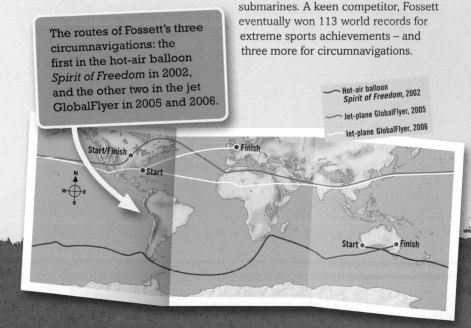

The routes of Fossett's three circumnavigations: the first in the hot-air balloon *Spirit of Freedom* in 2002, and the other two in the jet GlobalFlyer in 2005 and 2006.

Hot-air balloon
Spirit of Freedom, 2002

Jet-plane GlobalFlyer, 2005

Jet-plane GlobalFlyer, 2006

Start/Finish

Start

Finish

N
W E
S

Start   Finish

The problems of balloon flight

In the early 1990s, Fossett set himself a challenge. He was going to make the first solo flight around the world in a hot-air balloon. Fossett knew that this adventure would be extremely dangerous. Balloons can catch fire or be blown off course by storms. They can bounce and spin in air currents, or crash-land, or hit obstacles such as mountains.

Balloons are also uncomfortable for people flying in them! The air is so thin high up that pilots must wear oxygen masks so they can breathe. They also have to wear padded "spacesuits" to stop themselves freezing. As a solo pilot, Fossett had to stay awake night and day, catching brief snatches of sleep for just a few minutes at a time.

Balloon cabins are cramped, with no room for fresh food or lavatories. Fossett munched dried army rations and used a bucket and a bottle!

Fossett's record-breaking balloon flies high above Western Australia in 2002.

Spirit of Freedom

Five times, Fossett tried to fly around the world in a hot-air balloon. Five times, he failed. In 1998, on his fourth attempt, he was lucky to survive when the balloon plunged 8,840 metres (29,000 feet) into the sea. Finally, in 2002 – on his sixth bid to win the record – Fossett succeeded in his balloon *Spirit of Freedom*.

● TOOLS OF THE TRADE

Spirit of Freedom was taller than three buses parked end to end, and could reach a top speed of 322 kilometres (204 miles) per hour. On his around-the-world adventure, Fossett flew the balloon for 32,963 kilometres (20,385 miles) and stayed airborne for 14 days and 19 hours.

Designed and built for Fossett in the United States, GlobalFlyer was made of plastic and carbon fibre, with a single turbojet engine.

GlobalFlyer

Just three years after his balloon flight, Fossett was ready to try another circumnavigation: alone, non-stop, without refuelling. This time he was piloting an experimental plane called GlobalFlyer. Packed full of jet-propellant for the long flight, the plane could easily catch fire and explode.

TOOLS of the TRADE

GlobalFlyer's slim, streamlined wings measured 34.8 metres (114 feet) across – half as wide as a jumbo jet. However, the pilot's capsule was only 2.3 metres (7 feet) high, with the roaring jet engine frighteningly close behind. Fuel was stored in two huge "pods" on either side. The plane could travel at more than 460 kilometres (285 miles) per hour.

Cramped conditions

Fossett set off in 2005. He was strapped into the tiny pilot's capsule, with barely enough room to turn round or lie down. His only nourishment came from milk-based drinks, and his pilot's suit was fitted with waste-collection tubes. Although the plane had autopilot controls, Fossett dared not doze for more than a few minutes. There was also the risk that he might suffer from dangerous jet-lag and mental confusion.

Kansas to Kansas

He began his journey travelling eastwards from Salina, Kansas, USA. There was a frightening moment over the Pacific Ocean, when Fossett thought the GlobalFlyer was running short of fuel. But this proved to be a false alarm and Fossett flew on bravely. After 67 hours in the air, he finally arrived back in Kansas, having travelled 36,912 kilometres (22,936 miles). All alone, without stopping or refuelling, he had flown right around the world!

Fossett in the tiny cabin of GlobalFlyer. During the journey, he had to stay alert for days and nights without a break.

GlobalFlyer in the skies above Florida, ready to begin Fossett's third around-the-world race.

Don't stop trying!

Two circumnavigations were a fantastic achievement, but in 2006 Fossett climbed into the GlobalFlyer cockpit once again. His plan this time was to complete the longest non-stop solo flight ever made. Just over 76 hours later, he landed at Bournemouth, England, after a journey of 41,467 kilometres (25,766 miles). This was right around the world – and then some! No one had ever flown so far without stopping.

A future record?

Today, engineers and aircraft designers are working on a new type of plane, to try to beat Fossett's long-distance record. The Solar Impulse is a plane powered by sunlight and is already being tested in the United States.

A tragic end

The following year, in July 2007, Fossett was made a member of America's National Aviation Hall of Fame in Dayton, Ohio. In his speech of thanks, he promised to keep on breaking records. "I'm not done!" he declared.

"He led an extraordinary, absolutely remarkable life." **British businessman Richard Branson, paying tribute to his friend Steve Fossett**

Tragically, Fossett's life of adventure ended soon after. In September 2007, he took off to make an air survey of land in Nevada and California. Friends said he was searching for a site for his latest daring exploit: a bid to break the land-speed record in a super-fast car. But Fossett never returned. His crashed plane was found on a mountainside, with his remains close by.

After his circumnavigation successes, Fossett was often asked to speak at events, inspiring others to challenge themselves.

JASON LEWIS
MUSCLE POWER

After so many famous record-breaking adventures, was there any new way of travelling round the world? One man thought there was. His name was Jason Lewis, and he challenged himself to complete a circumnavigation using only human muscle power – "Expedition 360".

Lewis was born in Catterick, England, in 1967. As a young man, he was always busy: during the day he worked cleaning windows; at night, he played in a band. But, unlike the other adventurers in this book, he was not a trained, experienced athlete. He knew very little about boats or sailing. How would he survive?

Expedition 360

Together with his friend, the adventurer Steve Smith, Lewis set off in 1994. It took him the next 13 years to cover 74,842 kilometres (46,505 miles). He trudged on foot through dust and snow, cycled up icy mountains, paddled through wild waves in a kayak, sped along roads on inline skates, and crossed oceans in an amazing pedal-powered boat.

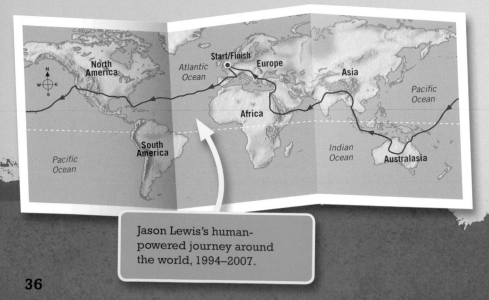

Jason Lewis's human-powered journey around the world, 1994–2007.

Dumitru Dan

The first person to circumnavigate the world on foot was Dumitru Dan from Romania. Between 1910 and 1923, Dan walked through 76 countries. He crossed the oceans by boat, of course, but he still kept walking all day long – up and down the deck. By the end of his adventure, he had worn through 497 pairs of shoes!

As part of his epic muscle-powered journey, Lewis travelled just over 32,268 kilometres (23,779 miles) by bicycle.

What's the point?

On his epic adventure, Lewis set three new records. But he also hoped that his travels would bring different peoples together, inspire respect for the environment, and help children learn about the world.

On the record-breaking Atlantic voyage, *Moksha* was almost overturned by a whale and very nearly wrecked on a coral reef.

Across the Atlantic

Lewis's adventure began in July 1994, when he cycled to the south coast of England. He and Smith crossed the Channel in their pedal-powered boat, *Moksha* (which means "freedom"), then cycled through France and Spain to Portugal. There, they boarded *Moksha* once again and headed for the United States.

The voyage lasted a gruelling 111 days. *Moksha* was tiny; just 8 metres (26 feet) long and 1.5 metres (4.5 feet) wide. Lewis and Smith took turns to pedal for four hours at a time, day and night. They ate porridge, soup, and stew made from a dried mix boiled up with water. Loneliness, seasickness, boredom, and painful sores made them miserable. Tiredness and stress led to quarrels. There was no privacy anywhere on board, even for going to the lavatory.

Disaster strikes!

After landing in Florida, USA, in January 1995, Lewis and Smith worked to earn money for fresh adventures. Lewis aimed to skate the 6,920 kilometres (4,300 miles) across the United States; Smith rode a bike. All went well until Lewis was hit by a car. Both his legs were broken, and it was nine months before he was well enough to continue the journey.

Together again, Lewis and Smith cycled south toward the vast Pacific Ocean. But stormy weather and dangerous seas forced them to change their plans. They cycled back to California, set off in *Moksha* in September 1998, and reached the Pacific island of Hawaii two months later.

"I'm overcome with the feeling that we are incredibly privileged to be here... The Pacific has been a great teacher for me."
Jason Lewis, 1998

Don't give up, don't give in

The later stages of Lewis's journey were just as tough as the first ones. After reaching Hawaii, Smith left the expedition. Lewis paddled on, alone, for 73 dangerous days. He fell ill, got confused, and began to talk to the fish! So, for the rest of his journey, he was often joined by friends or helpers. They reached Australia in 2000, Indonesia in 2005, and Tibet and western India in 2006. The next year, Lewis cycled through north Africa to Jordan, Syria, and Turkey – and then right across Europe.

"The first journey around the world by human power ... shows that ordinary people, filled with passion and helped by others, can accomplish the most extraordinary things."
Steve Smith

Lewis travelled alone in his kayak for part of the journey in Southeast Asia.

Lewis arrives back in London at the end of his amazing 13-year journey.

Along the way, Lewis risked meeting deadly snakes, sharks, crocodiles, and pirates. He faced extremes of heat and cold, hunger and thirst, delight and despair. He was nearly shipwrecked, accused of being a spy, and almost sent to prison. But he kept on going! At last, he paddled *Moksha* home to England on 6 October 2007. Cheering crowds were waiting. He had done it! It was a world first! A record!

Dare to dream

Just as important, Lewis had shared his amazing journey with people all around the world. He had given talks, visited schools, and set up websites so that anyone, anywhere, could follow his adventures. He wanted his trip to encourage people to hope, to dare – and, just like him, to follow their dreams.

TIMELINE

1519	Magellan (Portugal) and Elcano (Spain) set sail from Spain
1889	Nellie Bly (USA) travels around the world in 72 days
1895	Joshua Slocum (USA) sets off on first solo voyage around the world
1923	Dumitru Dan (Romania) completes his walk around the world
1966	Francis Chichester (UK) sets off on solo sea circumnavigation
1969	Robin Knox-Johnston (UK) completes first solo non-stop voyage around the world
1979	Ranulph Fiennes (UK) leads expedition to circumnavigate the globe, passing through North and South Poles
1986	Dick Rutan and Jeana Yaeger (USA) make first non-stop flight around the world
1987	Rick Hansen (Canada) completes "Man In Motion" circumnavigation by wheelchair
1988	Kay Cottee (Australia) completes first solo non-stop voyage around the world by a woman
1994	Jason Lewis (UK) sets off on the first circumnavigation of the globe by human power alone
2001	Ellen MacArthur (UK) becomes youngest person and fastest woman to sail solo around the world
2002	Steve Fossett (USA) makes first solo circumnavigation of the world by hot-air balloon
2005	Ellen MacArthur sets new speed record for sailing solo around the world; Steve Fossett makes first solo non-stop, non-refuelled flight around the world, in jet plane GlobalFlyer
2006	Steve Fossett completes longest-ever non-stop flight around the world in GlobalFlyer
2007	Jason Lewis completes first human-powered circumnavigation

Do you love to travel, see new places, and meet new people?

a Yes, I want to visit as many countries as I can.

b I like to travel, but prefer holiday trips to tough expeditions.

c I prefer to see the world through books, computers, and TV.

Are you strong and healthy, with lots of energy? Which sports do you play?

a I'm active! I get restless if I spend too long sitting down. Running and rowing are my favourite sports, and I want to learn to climb mountains.

b I'm healthy, but I'm not especially strong. I love swimming and cycling.

c I don't like sports, except watching it on TV.

Can you cope with extreme weather, rough country, loneliness, accidents, and injuries?

a I know survival skills and first aid, and I can keep a cool head in a crisis.

b I'm fairly hardy, but I don't know how I'd cope all alone in an emergency.

c I like to stay indoors when it's cold. The sight of blood makes me faint!

Are you determined to finish a task once you've begun it?

a I like a challenge and get a thrill out of solving problems.

b I try to finish projects if I can.

c I usually give up when things get difficult.

Are you afraid to take risks or venture into the unknown?

a I long to have adventures! Good explorers can manage risks sensibly.

b I'd like to see more of the world, but the risks rather frighten me.

c I can't understand why people risk their lives to go exploring.

ANSWERS:

Mostly a: You're strong, tough, brave, determined, and keen to find out more. You'd be a good circumnavigator.

Mostly b: You might manage a circumnavigation, and you might even enjoy it. But shorter adventure trips might be better for you to begin with.

Mostly c: Circumnavigation is not for you at the moment. But perhaps you need to get out more and find out what you're missing!

GLOSSARY

autopilot set of automatic controls used to guide an aircraft without the help of a human pilot

carbon fibre very strong, lightweight material made of extremely thin fibres bonded together

crevasse deep, often hidden, crack in an ice-sheet or glacier

endurance being able to keep active for a long time

Equator imaginary line drawn around Earth at its widest point

exploit daring adventure

fatigued very tired

frostbite serious damage to skin and flesh, caused by extreme cold

glacier slow-moving sheet of ice

ice-floe mass of ice, like a small island, floating in the sea

ice-sheet thick layer of ice covering land; in parts of Antarctica the ice-sheet is 4.7 kilometres (3 miles) deep

jet lag feeling of tiredness and confusion caused by travelling quickly across several time zones

jet-propellant special fuel designed to power jet engines

lines of longitude imaginary lines running north to south on Earth's surface, used to measure distances east or west from a fixed point at Greenwich, England

marathon long-distance running race of 42 kilometres (26 miles)

patron someone who gives money or other types of support to an activity or organization

pioneering using new ways of doing things

propeller type of fan connected to an engine and fixed to a ship's hull; as the propeller turns, it pushes the ship through the water

rudder moveable paddle, made of metal or wood, used to steer a ship

scurvy disease caused by lack of Vitamin C, a substance found in fresh fruit; humans need this vitamin to stay alive

skidoo vehicle designed to travel on snow and ice, with tracks instead of wheels

snow-bridge layers of wind-blown snow covering a crevasse, like a bridge

solo alone, without any help

streamlined specially shaped to limit wind resistance, to allow higher speeds to be reached

summit highest point

trimaran yacht with three hulls next to each other

FIND OUT MORE

Books

Ellen MacArthur (Sports Files), Claire Throp (Raintree, 2009)

Ferdinand Magellan, Circumnavigating the World, Katherine Bailey (Crabtree Books, 2005)

Go Wild! 101 Things To Do Outdoors Before You Grow Up, Fiona Danks and Jo Schofield (Frances Lincoln, 2009)

Nellie Bly: Journalist (Women of Achievement), John Bankston (Checkmark Books, 2011)

Racing on the Wind: Steve Fossett (Shockwave: Life Stories), Laura Layton Strom (Children's Press, 2007)

Websites

www.expedition360.com
Meet Jason Lewis and the team that helped him on his amazing human-powered circumnavigation.

news.bbc.co.uk/1/hi/sci/tech/4316599.stm
Read about Steve Fossett's adventures and his plane GlobalFlyer.

news.bbc.co.uk/sport1/hi/other_sports/ sailing/4192517.stm
Follow Ellen MacArthur's record-breaking voyage.

www.rickhansen.com/Who-We-Are/About-Rick-Hansen/Man-In-Motion-World-Tour/A-Day-on-the-Road.aspx

Join Rick Hansen as he wheels round the world.

www.transglobe-expedition.org

The place to find out about Ranulph Fiennes's Transglobe Expedition.

Further research

Which circumnavigation described in this book would you like to have taken part in? Make a list and give your reasons.

Use books and the internet to find out more about Ellen MacArthur's boat or Steve Fossett's plane. Explain how technology helped MacArthur and Fossett succeed in their adventures.

Imagine that you are a journalist, sent to interview one of the around-the-world-adventurers in this book. What questions would you like to ask them?

Are there any adventure sports, such as rowing or climbing, that you would like to learn? Do some research and maybe ask your sports teacher.

INDEX

air, circumnavigation by 28–35

Amundsen, Roald 11
Antarctica 12–13
Arctic 10, 11, 14–15

balloons 7, 29–31, 42
Benjamin Bowring 12, 14, 15
Bethune, Pete 6
Bly, Nellie 9, 42
Bothie 14
Branson, Richard 7, 35
Burton, Charlie 12–15

Castorama 26–7
Charles, Prince 10
Chichester, Sir Francis 23, 42
Cottee, Kay 23, 42
cycling 36–40

Dan, Dumitru 37, 42
disabled circumnavigators 16–21

Earth 6
Earthrace 6
Elcano, Juan 4, 42
Everest 14
Expedition 360 36–41, 42

Fiennes, Ranulph 10–15, 42
Fiennes, Virginia (Ginny) 10, 11, 14

flight, non-stop 28–35, 42
Fossett, Steve 28–35, 42
Fox, Terry 18

GlobalFlyer 29, 32–4, 42
Goss, Pete 25

Hansen, Rick 16–21, 42
hot-air balloons 7, 29–31, 42

inline skating 36, 39

Joyon, Francis 26

kayaking 36, 40
Kingfisher 24, 25
Knox-Johnston, Sir Robin 23, 42

Lewis, Jason 36–41, 42
Lord Nelson 21

MacArthur, Ellen 22–7, 42
Magellan, Ferdinand 4, 7, 42
"Man In Motion World Tour" 16–21, 42
Moksha 38, 41
muscle power 36–41, 42

North Pole 10, 11, 14–15, 42

Pan-American Wheelchair Games 16
Paralympic Games 17
pedal-powered boat 36, 38, 41
polar exploration 10–15

Rutan, Dick 28, 42

sea, circumnavigation by
  Earthrace 7
  Ellen MacArthur 22–7, 42
  Francis Chichester 23, 42
  Jason Lewis 36–41, 42
  Joshua Slocum 5, 7, 42
  Lord Nelson 21
  Robin Knox-Johnston 23, 42
Shepard, Oliver 12–14
Slocum, Joshua 5, 7, 42
Smith, Steve 36–40
Solar Impulse 34
South Pole 11, 12–13, 42
Spirit of Freedom 29–31

tall ships 21
Transglobe Expedition 10–15

Vendée Globe 24–5
Verne, Jules, *Around the World in Eighty Days* 8, 9